Metropolitan Borough of Cal  D1581404

LEISURE SERVICES DEPARTMENT

LIBRARIES DIVISION

Books should be returned on or before the last date shown below. Any book **not required by another reader** may be renewed.

To renew, give your library membership number.

DATE DUE FOR RETURN

34 171 721

Stan Kielty, scrum-half hero of the 1950s, who revelled alongside Halifax's ferocious pack of forwards.

IMAGES
of Sport

HALIFAX
RUGBY LEAGUE CLUB
THE FIRST 100 YEARS

Compiled by
Andrew Hardcastle

TEMPUS

First published 1999
Copyright © Andrew Hardcastle, 1999

Tempus Publishing Limited
The Mill, Brimscombe Port,
Stroud, Gloucestershire, GL5 2QG

ISBN 0 7524 1831 9

Typesetting and origination by
Tempus Publishing Limited
Printed in Great Britain by
Midway Clark Printing, Wiltshire

A selection of present and forthcoming sports titles from Tempus Publishing:

Headingley Rugby Voices
Hunslet Rugby League Club
Leeds Rugby League Club
Sheffield Eagles Rugby League Club
St Helens Rugby League Club
Warrington Rugby League Club

Ken Dean ready to pass to Billy Mather against Leigh at Thrum Hall in 1957.

Contents

LES WHITE (Halifax).

A caricature of second-row forward Les White, a 1949 signing from Wigan.

Introduction

Halifax Rugby Club originated in 1873, although the first match was not played until November 1874. For the first twenty-two years it played Rugby Union, as did every club at that time, but in 1895 was one of the twenty-two clubs to break away to form the Northern Union. The new game changed its name to Rugby League in 1922.

This book does not claim to be a detailed record of the club. Several club histories, most recently *The Thrum Hall Story* (1986), have filled that role. It does, however, follow a chronological line through the club's first 100 seasons, highlighting the many good times and some of the bad. The rules and fixture formats have regularly changed over the years, as has the number of trophies available in any one season. There has always been a Championship of one form or another, and the Challenge Cup was introduced in the 1896/97 season. The Yorkshire Cup was added in 1905/06, followed by a Yorkshire League in 1907/08. The latter was a trophy for the Yorkshire team which fared best in matches against teams from its own county in the normal run of League fixtures; it had replaced an earlier Yorkshire Senior Competition and lasted until 1970. In more recent times came the BBC2 Floodlit Competition (1965) and the John Player Trophy (1971/72).

Throughout the first 100 years, Halifax played in blue and white hooped shirts, initially with black shorts but for the most part with white. As these images show, however, there have been a variety of different change strips. Hopefully, the photographs and other memorabilia will bring back memories for those who have followed the club for many years, and show others what the ground, the players, and the game as a whole, were like in the times before they were born.

Acknowledgements

The photographs and other illustrations in this book are from the author's private collection, which has been built up over the years thanks to the help of a succession of players, officials and fans. A great debt is owed to the photographers of the past, particularly those of the *Halifax Evening Courier*, who will have been responsible for several of them. The *Courier* has also helped out with the provision of copies of photographs from their own archives.

In particular I would like to thank my son Nicholas, who transferred the hand-written work onto disk for submission to the publishers. Others who have helped, perhaps without realising it in some cases, are: Bill Berry, Nigel Colbeck, John Cox, Don Craven, Trevor Delaney, Betty Dyson, Robert Gate, Stephen Gee, John Grecian, David Hanson, Mike Flynn, Les Hoole, H. Milnes, Jim Moran, Tom Houston, Howard Jeffrey, Ken Jones, Brian Robinson, Keith Sutcliffe, Tony Thwaites, Brenda Whiteley and Anne Wilkinson. If there is anyone I have inadvertently forgotten, I offer my sincere apologies.

Andrew Hardcastle
August 1999

Dave Rayner, Ronnie James, Terry Fogerty and Stuart Kelley defend their line in the late 1960s.

One

Rugby Union Days

The inauspicious advertisement in the centre of this extract from the *Halifax Guardian* of Saturday 1 November 1873 heralded the birth of the Halifax club. It was placed by five friends, members of the Fourth West Yorkshire Rifle Volunteers (note the advertisement below), who had seen reports of football matches elsewhere in Yorkshire and fancied forming a team in Halifax. It was not the most successful of appeals as only eight people turned up, but the club was formed regardless.

The Hanson Lane ground, 1876/86. Finding a suitable ground was a recurring problem in the first couple of years. After the first venue in King Cross Street, the home of Trinity Cricket Club, was lost to building work, the club tried Ovenden United's cricket field on Cousin Lane for a couple of matches. There followed a short spell on Savile Park, ahead of a ground share arrangement with Trinity again, at their new field on the corner of Hanson Lane and Thrum Hall Lane. This location boasted a small pavilion, although the grandstand shown in this 1885 sketch was not erected until 1877. Some of the buildings in the background, near Queens Road, are still standing.

One of the early great players was George Thomson, a local youngster who made his debut on Christmas Eve, 1875. This drawing depicts him in his England cap and shirt, for he became the club's first international player in 1878, appearing nine times in all for his country.

The team rapidly became very successful. The 1877/78 season saw the introduction of the Yorkshire Cup and Halifax became its first-ever winners, beating York in the final at Holbeck. The illustration shows some of the leading players and officials. The cup, seen in the centre, is still presented each year by the Yorkshire Rugby Football Union.

There were no mementoes for individual players at the 1877/78 final, so Halifax members and supporters subscribed towards gold medals, which were presented a few weeks later by Alderman J.T. Riley. The medal in the photograph was for half-back James Robinson.

Albert Wood was a talented player who made his debut in 1880 and appeared among both backs and forwards for the club. In the 1883/84 season he became Halifax's second England international when he played as a forward against Ireland at Lansdowne Road, Dublin. Wood also made ten appearances for the Yorkshire county side, but emigrated to Australia in 1884.

In 1895, J.C. Trott had a collection of poems and songs published by the Guardian Printing Works, George Street. It included this poem based on an 1887 Halifax victory over local rivals Bradford, a team perceived by some at the time to be a 'gentleman's team'. Halifax themselves were always seen as a working-class side.

"THE GOOD TIME COMING."
A HINT FOR HALIFAX.

Bradford and Wakefield (elated by their recent successes) : Ay, lad; ay, lad; put up thy shutters and dry off a bit. Hedn't 'ta botter stick this on thy winders an' all, thinks ta?
Halifax (cheerily) : Oh, ye may laugh nah, but just wait a bit till I've organised my establishment a trifle, an' then see if I don't give ye all as big a lickin' as ivver I did afore!

This cartoon appeared in a periodical called *The Yorkshireman* in 1883, following away defeats at Bradford and Wakefield. The message was prophetic, for Halifax quickly returned to winning ways and continued to be a leading side throughout their years in the Rugby Union.

THE HALIFAX FOOTBALL FIVE.
(From Photographs by Messrs. Brown, Barnes & Bell, of Kirkgate, Bradford, and Commercial Street, Leeds.)

ALBERT WOOD.

GEORGE THOMSON.

J. DODD *(Captain)*.

J. CROSSLAND,

E. BUCKLEY.

The Yorkshireman carried regular news of Halifax and other clubs from the area, sometimes with illustrations. These drawings show five of Halifax's numerous county selections during the 1880s, including internationals Thomson and Wood. Jimmy Dodd was one of the club's all-time greats in a career that lasted from 1876 until 1893. Crossland was a long-serving forward (1879-1887), while 'Little' Buckley was a tiny half-back (of just 5ft 2in) who won the admiration of the Halifax fans for ten years from 1880.

Halifax were Yorkshire Cup winners again in 1886, beating Bradford in the final at Cardigan Fields in Leeds. From left to right, back row: Stansfield, Baldwin. Fourth row: Murgatroyd, T. Watson, Pollard, Crossland. Third row: W. Wood, Dodd, T. Scarborough, Welsh, Dennis. Second row: Albutt, Buckley, Parker, Clowes. Front row: Millar, Brown (secretary), E. Scarborough, Webster.

Early team photographs were usually taken at the cricket-field side of the pavilion on a balcony, which was later demolished. This one dates from around 1890 and, although all the players cannot be identified, the group includes outstanding individuals like Ike Webster (nephew of Samuel Webster who founded Webster's Brewery), Fred Firth and Jim Knowles.

Since the very early days, Halifax had always fielded an 'A' or reserve side. In 1892 it won the Halifax Infirmary Charity Cup, a competition for local teams which survives to this day as the Halifax Amateur Rugby League Challenge Cup. Halifax 'A' were also winners on several other occasions. Amongst those in this photograph are George Milnes (last player at the back on the right), and a young Archie Rigg (front left).

Rugby Union action from the 1890s. The line-out is from a game that took place at Fartown, Huddersfield, watched by a large crowd, although the Halifax man at the front seems more intent on looking at the photographer rather than the ball.

In the 1890s rugby was the dominant sport in Yorkshire, far exceeding soccer in popularity. J. Baines of Bradford saw an opening in the market and produced cards for youngsters to collect. This one features Halifax's Fred Firth, a star wingman who had been recruited from Brighouse Rangers in 1890. He played 20 times for Yorkshire under Rugby Union rules, and 3 times for England in 1894 against Scotland, Ireland and Wales, then made 6 appearances for the Yorkshire Northern Union side after 1895.

Another producer of collectors' cards was W.N. Sharpe, also of Bradford, who issued several to commemorate Halifax's winning of the Yorkshire Cup in both 1893 and 1894. The player on this card is the captain, Otis Fletcher.

The Thrum Hall pavilion, built in 1886, was an imposing structure, with an enclosure for 'players and officials only' to its front. The result being displayed on the scoreboard perhaps dates the photograph at 1893, for that was the outcome of the final home game of the 1892/93 season against Kendal Hornets. The fence surrounding the playing area has seating attached to it, and the Main Stand as yet has no roof.

The cricket side of the pavilion also looked quite different when it was first built. The towers, with balcony between, were later removed, as was the seating below in more recent times. The rugby club's boardroom was situated in the middle room of the tower on the right and is probably the only boardroom with a magnificent view of a cricket field.

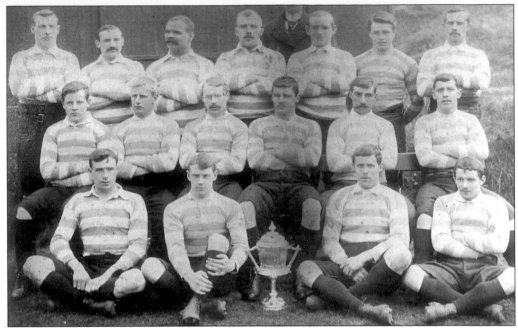

The 1893/94 Yorkshire Cup final success, when Castleford were beaten 39-6 at Leeds, was Halifax's fifth – a new record for the game. The players shown are, from left to right, back row: Jack Riley, Webster, Wilson, Mellor, Knowles, Fookes, Bromwich. Middle row: Wheelwright, Robertshaw, Jackson, Fletcher, Firth, Bottomley. Front row: Rigg, Arnold, Dickenson, A. Chorley.

The 1894/95 season was to be Halifax's last as a Rugby Union side. Like other leading sides in Yorkshire and Lancashire they were becoming disillusioned with the game's rulers at Twickenham – particularly their views on broken-time payments to players – and finally decided to break away. This team group was taken for *The People* at Batley on 15 September 1894.

Two

1895-1918

The vast majority of the players were happy to stay with the club following the 1895 breakaway, even though they were forsaking their chances of international rugby. One who would surely have achieved this was Archie Rigg, who won county honours several times in both codes. On the left is a Baines card with Rigg wearing his Yorkshire Rugby Union cap and shirt, while on the right he is featured on an Ogden's Guinea Gold cigarette card from 1899, wearing the Yorkshire Northern Union shirt

HALIFAX, MAY 9TH, 1896.

SIR,

The ANNUAL GENERAL MEETING of the HALIFAX CRICKET AND FOOTBALL CLUB will be held in the MECHANICS' HALL, HALIFAX, on THURSDAY, MAY 21st, at 7-30 p.m., at which your attendance is respectfully requested.

MAJOR BROWN, *Secretary.*

The Committee have pleasure in presenting their Report and Balance Sheet to the Members. The Season has been a most eventful one in the Club's history. Your Committee thought it desirable to introduce the Association Game, and eventually made arrangements with the Association Club then existing in Halifax, to join the Halifax Club. We also became affiliated with the Football Association of England; and are pleased to state, the team under the Captaincy of Mr. Cattell, has been fairly successful in its matches, and will no doubt, next season, show still further improvement.

The Cricket Season was an exceptionally good one, the weather was favourable, and the performances of your teams highly creditable and satisfactory. A very pleasing feature in connection with Cricket is the increased interest which has been taken in this branch of sport, both by the members and the public generally.

The Committee regret that the Bowling Green does not receive the support that is desirable, the Green being considered one of the best in the County.

The 19th Annual Athletic Festival was held under most favourable circumstances, and the attendance one of the largest on record. The thanks of all are due to Mr. S. Foster (Hon. Sec.) and the Sports Committee for the increased popularity of our Festival, which is now classed one of the leading meetings of the North of England.

In consequence of the drastic new rules drafted by the English Rugby Union, the Senior Clubs of Lancashire and Yorkshire decided to resign Membership of the English Rugby Union and and also of their respective County Unions. It was decided to establish a Northern Rugby Union, and your Committee after due and full consideration, joined the new organization.

The formation of the N.F.U. entailed upon the team a much heavier programme than usual; taking into account the calibre of the teams to be met, and that each match being a competition match, it undoubtedly rendered the strain upon the players more severe than ever before experienced. Although our team failed to attain the object of their ambition—the Championship of the Northern Rugby Union—the season has been the most successful in the history of the Club. We have again had the honour of having three men chosen for all the County Matches, viz:—Messrs. Rigg, Firth, and Riley, and we must congratulate Mr. Rigg on his appointment as Captain of the Yorkshire team.

During the year the grounds and property of the Club have been kept in an efficient state of repair, and after meeting all the accounts coming against the financial year there is a Balance of Income over Expenditure of £279 16s. 7½d.

The CRICKET ELEVEN played 29 Matches, of which 11 were won, 8 lost, and 10 drawn; the total runs scored by Halifax was 3432, average of 14·102 runs per wicket; while their opponents scored 2734, an average of 11·160 runs per wicket.

THE SECOND ELEVEN played 25 Matches, of which 15 were won, 4 lost, and 6 drawn.

The FOOTBALL TEAM have take part in 42 matches, of which 30 were won, 7 lost, and 5 drawn.

	Goals.	Tries.	Points.
Halifax	41	42	312
Opponents ...	22	14	139
	19	28	173

The "A" TEAM have taken part in 20 Matches, of which 11 were won, 7 lost and 3 drawn.

Halifax "A" ...	27	27	194
Opponents ...	10	14	92
	17	13	102

During the year ending April 30th, the Committee have been summoned 54 times :—

T. BOWER	47	T. SUNDERLAND	47	JOE NICHOLL	38
F. BEDFORD	34	I. H. SKINNER	28	H. WILKINSON	27
		Elected June 10th.			
J. H. BROMWICH	26	F. CROSSLEY	40	H. TURNER	14
S. FOSTER	46	I. WEBSTER	36	R. WILKINSON	33
F. FIRTH	20	J. J. PATCHETT	39	R. E. OLROYD	43
J. H. CROSSLAND	41	M. PATCHETT	41	A. BINGLEY	40
J. DODD	36	E. SCARBOROUGH ...	41		

The first five Members retire this year.

Members must produce their Cards on entering the Meeting.

Members' Subscriptions are now due, and must be paid to MAJOR BROWN, at the Registered Office, 1, Argyle Street (off Waterhouse Street).

The breakaway from the Rugby Football Union was not all about money, but it was high on the list of importance. The players were not paid – professionalism was immediately declared illegal – other than as a recompense for missing time at work, but the clubs hoped to rake in cash from

Halifax Cricket & Football Club.

Dr.   REVENUE ACCOUNT.   **Cr.**

Season 1894-5. £ s. d.	EXPENDITURE.		Season 1895-6. £ s. d.	£ s. d.	Season 1894-5. £ s. d.	INCOME.	Season 1895-6. £ s. d.
298 10 6	To Athletic Sports			278 8 6	285 13 6	By Athletic Sports	346 6 8
	,, WAGES AS UNDER:—				8 0 6	,, County Cricket	
141 5 6	Groundsmen	129 18 0			11 12 6	,, Discounts	8 2 8
127 2 6	Professional Cricketers	180 15 1				By SUBSCRIPTIONS, AS UNDER:—	
74 12 6	Gatekeepers	85 0 0			1042 13 6	,, 1634 members & 148 Subscribers	
140 0 0	Secretary	140 0 0				1403 do. 155 do 914 10 0	
12 15 3	Police	15 17 11				1 New Life Members (Total 46) 10 10 0	925 0 0
58 16 6	Sundries	24 13 3			122 7 0	,, Rents	121 17 0
554 12 3			576 4 3		1220 1 11	,, Gate and Stands	1852 0 4
					486 8 3	,, Balance of Expenditure over Income	
	To MAINTENANCE OF GROUND AS UNDER:—						
13 15 10	Wages	10 7 0					
18 4 8	Horse Work	20 14 2					
7 17 4	Materials, &c.,	64 5 6					
8 12 9	Coals	8 7 7					
91 6 5	Clearing Snow & cost of Straw, &c.	150 16 9					
15 12 9	Alterations						
6 10 0	Sundries per Groundsman	5 18 3					
8 14 9	Washing	14 5 2					
170 14 6			274 14 5				
	To REPAIRS AND RENEWALS AS UNDER:—						
13 7 0	Mason						
34 4 11½	Joiner	75 14 0					
13 11 2	Painter	0 16 10					
2 13 3	Plumber	20 4 5					
	Plasterer	10 0 1					
10 18 10	Ironwork	22 3 10					
6 18 7	Sundries	0 3 8					
			129 2 10				
19 10 0	Washhouse						
610 2 8	New Stand						
711 6 5½							
89 3 7	Printing and Stationery	104 9 9					
26 7 6	Billposting	28 7 4					
7 18 4	Advertising	12 16 11					
34 19 8½	Stamps, Telegrams. &c.	30 6 1½					
158 9 1½			176 0 1½				
	To DINNERS, TEAS, ETC., AS UNDER:—						
112 14 2	Visiting Teams	122 6 11					
68 8 1	Players away	96 7 11					
25 5 8	Refreshments on Ground	55 11 2					
206 7 11			274 6 0				
349 17 4	To Travelling Expenses		367 10 8				
25 15 6	,, Delegates, Deputations, &c.		31 0 3				
66 10 5¼	,, Outfitting		112 10 3				
136 6 6	,, Rent, Rates, Gas and Water		141 8 11				
36 19 11½	,, Referees, &c.		56 12 7				
32 16 2	,, Medical Aid		31 9 8				
70 0 0	,, Insurance—Players		74 13 8				
3 0 0	,, ,, Pavilion		3 0 0				
15 12 6	,, Subscriptions to other Clubs		49 0 1				
11 17 6	,, Talent Money		16 7 6				
1 1 0	,, Registration of Telegraphic Address		1 1 0				
50 2 9	,, Photographs, Medals, &c.		16 13 0				
6 1 4	,, Sundries		11 2 1				
20 0 0	,, Donations to other Clubs		68 11 10				
4 6 8	,, Legal Expenses						
3 3 0	,, Hire of Hall for Meeting		2 2 0				
4 4 8	,, Petty Cash per Secretary		2 3 9				
70 7 6	,, Office Furnishing						
11 10 4	,, Bad Debt						
157 3 3	,, Interest		160 10 8				
	,, Auditing		5 0 0				
	,, Broken Time Allowance		113 16 0				
	,, Balance of Income over expenditure		279 16 7½				
3176 17 2			3253 6 8				
			£3176 17 2		£3253 6 8		

BALANCE SHEET, 30th APRIL, 1896.

April 30th, 1895.	LIABILITIES.	£ s. d.	£ s. d.	April 30th, 1895.	ASSETS.	£ s. d.	£ s. d.
7 0 0	To Amount owing by club	7 0 0		171 8 3	By Loose Plant Estimated	171 8 3	
160 0 0	,, ,, ,, Bank			7792 14 3	,, Thrum Hall Estate	7792 14 3	
4000 0 0	,, ,, ,, Mortgage	4000 0 0		2 13 7	,, Cash in hand	0 8 5½	
	SURPLUS.				,, Cash in bank	122 1 9	
3799 16 1	As per balance sheet April 30th, 1895	3799 16 1					
	Income over expenditure per revenue account as above	279 16 7½					
			4079 12 8½				
7966 16 1			8086 12 8½	7966 16 1			£8086 12 8½

MAY 9th, 1896,   Examined with Books and Vouchers, and found correct, May 9th, 1896,

MAJOR BROWN, Secretary.   JAMES DUFF & WHITHAM, CHARTERED ACCOUNTANTS, HALIFAX.

increased gates. Halifax got them as a result of a very successful team, which finished the first season as runners-up to Manningham. The above revenue account and balance sheet for 1895/96 reveals a profit of £280, which was double the secretary's annual wage.

At the end of the nineteenth century, Northern Union teams were playing in county leagues. The team of 1899/1900 finished third in what was called the Yorkshire Senior Competition. From left to right, back row: Skinner (secretary), Kitchen (reporter), Mallinson, Jack Riley, Dewhirst, Tyson (president), Langhorn, Jones, Nicholl, Bartle, Dickinson (kitman), Midgley (trainer). Middle row: Wood, Rigg, Winskill, Morton, Kitson, Newell. Front row: Dickenson, Helliwell, J. Morley, Stoyle, Arnold, Nettleton, Cookson.

ROVERS v HALIFAX.

Early Northern Union action from a match at Hull KR's Craven Street ground, which saw service between 1896 and 1922. Halifax's first visit there was in January 1900, although this photograph could date from a couple of years after that.

September 28, 1901. SHUREY'S ILLUSTRATED. 13

FAMOUS FOOTBALL TEAMS AND PLAYERS.

A SHORT EPITOME OF PREVIOUS SUCCESSES AND PRESENT PROSPECTS. BY IVANHOE.

HALIFAX FOOTBALL CLUB.

MEMBERS OF THE NEWLY-FORMED NORTHERN RUGBY UNION.

The Halifax Cricket and Football Club, to give the organisation its full title, has commenced a new era of its existence by being included in the new Northern Union League. The club cannot boast of so lengthy a history as can some of its county contemporaries, but since the formation, in 1873, it has played a most honourable part in the handling game, and has generally managed to hold its own against strong opponents from all parts of the United Kingdom. At the inception of the club, matters were really difficult to arrange, yet it was really the result of a quiet conversation among some members of the Halifax Athletic Club that the idea of a football club first originated. The *Halifax Guardian*, of November 1st, 1873, was the medium employed to organise the project, and the following notice was inserted in its columns by Mr S. Duckitt: "Persons desirous of forming a football and athletic club are requested to meet on Thursday next, at 8.30 p.m., at the Upper George Hotel." The response was meagre, but among those present were Major Brown, S. Duckitt, A. Walsh, A. and J. Nicholls, and J. Pearson. Mr. Walsh was elected captain, and Mr. A. Nicholls hon. sec. With a membership of ten the first game was played on the Trinity Cricket Ground on December 6th of the same year. The next season found the club prospering, with its numbers enlarged to sixteen. Seven matches were played, and, considering it was only the second year of the club's existence, the record of 3 victories, 1 defeat, and 3 drawn games was not at all bad, considering that their opponents were Wakefield Trinity, Wakefield and Leeds Athletic. This success tended to draw support, and when season 1875-6 was opened it was under stronger auspices. Deprived of the use of the Trinity cricket ground, a venue was found on Skirtcoat Moor, and as the pitch was open to the public free of charge, great crowds used to assemble and watch the play. This was really the commencement of the club's public patronage, and there is no doubt that through these complimentary performances the interest in football grew, for Halifax soon afterwards could reckon on as big a following as any club in Yorkshire. The players were an enthusiastic lot, and had to find all their own outfit and pay travelling expenses, the Skirtcoat assembly contributing no income to the club. Among the crowd there was one George Thomson, a regular attendant at the games, and he it was who was responsible for raising the tone of the team, and during his career as a player he improved the standard of the play and put the club among the first flight of Rugby organisations. In 1876-7, the football club amalgamated with the brethren of the bat and ball, and a new ground was opened, at Hanson Lane, as the result. This eventually became a noted venue, and several high-class contests took place thereon, it being chosen for North v. South and Champion County v. Rest of England fixtures. It was here also where Lancastrian rivals were first met, Swinton and Broughton Rangers, out of the present-day clubs, being entertained, the venue continuing to serve for headquarters until the present enclosure at Thrum Hall was purchased and laid out. The Cup career of the club has been one of the most successful that any supporter could wish for, and the Yorkshire Cup—now but a shadow as compared to its importance a decade ago—was won by the Halifax fifteen in its first year of competition, the men then being led to victory by Alfred Walsh, and Bradford were their opponents in the final. The trophy was captured next in 1886, and on three other occasions—1888, 1893, and 1894—the club had the honour of holding it, creating a record by winning twice in succession. The season 1886-87, in fact, was one of the most successful that the Halifax Club has ever known; for, in addition to winning the Yorkshire Cup, the team captured the Charity Cup, while the summer representatives carried off the Cricket Challenge Cup.

When the break between the Rugby Union and the northern clubs, over the broken time question, occurred in 1895, resulting in the formation of the Northern Union, Halifax, like their principal neighbours, took the side of the new body, but the team did nothing startling in either competition. J. A. Rigg was the skipper under the new auspices, and it must be a great honour to him to again be requested to take the reins during the present season. However, since the initiation of the new body, Halifax has been one of the most consistent teams, and their drawing powers have always been recognised. The team, after passing through a not too satisfactory season in 1895, improved matters during the following year by gaining third place among their Yorkshire brethren in the table, gaining 40 points for the 30 games, Brighouse Rangers and Manningham being placed before them, with 48 and 46 points respectively. In 1897-8 the position was not maintained, for Hunslet, Bradford and Batley preceded Halifax in the statistics, and 35 points were gained. A further falling-off was noticeable at the end of the following season, for only half the programme of 30 games was won, and the remaining moiety lost, necessitating the position of eighth in the Yorkshire section. Season 1899-00 found the team much improved, and with a record of 20 games won, 7 lost, and 3 drawn, Halifax were again able to get back to the position of third, after scoring 26 goals and 47 tries against 18 goals and 28 tries. Last season was the most successful one the team has had since the Yorkshire Cup days, for they ran their powerful neighbours of Bradford a rare race for premier honours, the Park Avenue lot eventually getting home first. However, the Halifax record was a splendid one, winning, as the team did, 22 out of 30 games, losing 5, the remainder being drawn. The scoring proclivities were very prolific, as 48 goals and 71 tries were counted against 21 goals and 35 tries.

When the present season opened, it was anticipated that the prospects of maintaining good position in the statistics were of a roseate hue; but disappointments against Broughton Rangers and Runcorn have opened the eyes of the Committee as to their needs. It has been obvious to all that training had not been indulged in with the same vigour in Yorkshire as in the neighbouring counties, and want of condition has told its tale.

Still, the Northern Union League is a new organisation, and doubtless the name of Halifax will be written large and often among its annals before many seasons have passed over. Certainly the Committee did not spare their efforts to obtain the coveted talent, and as they said: "If Halifax lads are good enough for Huddersfield, Rochdale Hornets and Manningham, surely there is no reason why we should overlook their claims." However, practically the whole of last season's exponents were signed on. Of the new blood, the chief acquisition is Albert Brown, of Cardiff, who has the reputation of being one of the most promising half-backs in South Wales. For two seasons he was first reserve for Durham County, and is a very tricky player. Others available for duty behind the pack are Morley, Nettleton, Akroyd, who played with the second team last year, and King, a Southowram lad, who promises well. Figuring on the three quarter line, there are still to call upon: Rigg (captain), Nichol, Mallinson, and Fred Firth, the same quartette as last season. Some new backs from local clubs have been persuaded to cast in their lot, of whom there are Devitt, late of Halifax Crescent; Doherty, of Shibden; R. Wood, a chip off the old block; Blakey, of Coley; and D. Pugh, of Luddendenfoot. Arnold, who has done good service in the team in previous years, still retains a place. With regard to the pack, the club is well off for men, and in addition to the

J. A. RIGG (CAPT.). JOE RILEY. G. KITSON. T. NICHOL. J. E. JONES. W. KNOWLES. W. MORTON. J. BARTLE. E. H. LANGHAM. J. SWINBACK. J. ARNOLD. E. HELLIWELL. R. S. WINSKILL. A. G. BROWN. J. RILEY.

LOUIS M. MAGEE (Ireland and London Irish R.F.C.).

The green isle has often distinguished itself through its proud sons at the Rugby Union game, the determined nature of its representatives ever being a national trait. Chiefly among the pack has this quality been demonstrated, but there are at present, and have been in the past, giants towering above the ruck of moderate players. Such a one is the subject of our sketch, one of the best half-backs of the last decade. Louis Magee was born twenty-six years ago, and was educated at Clongowes Wood College, where he early made a mark, both as a promising footballer and cricketer. Leaving school in 1891, he joined the Bective Rangers, a club with which his elder brother, J. T. Magee, an ex-220 yards and quarter-mile champion of Ireland, was identified. Louis was selected for Leinster against Ulster in 1894, and the following season secured International honours. He went to South Africa with the Rugby Union in 1896, and it was his great desire to again visit the theatre of war, but family matters prevailed. Of late years Mr. Magee has been almost wholly identified with Irish International football, and has generally acted as mentor to his countrymen. On the formation of the national club in London his services were much sought after, and he has even assisted Middlesex in its County Championship programme. As a player, Magee is very cool and resourceful, shining most in the attack. He runs fast, kicks and dodges well, passes unselfishly and with considerable judgment, and is a deadly shot at goal either from a place or a drop. He will again lead the London Irish in this season's games.

Photo by Lafayette, Dublin.

LOOK OUT FOR GAINSBOROUGH TRINITY NEXT WEEK.

Fourteen clubs left the county leagues to form an early version of Superleague in the 1901/02 season, Halifax finishing fifth. The players were featured alongside pictures from the Boer War in *Shurey's Illustrated*, an A3-sized magazine that cost one penny. The Fleet Street editor managed to spoil the effect by including a Rugby Union player prominently in the centre.

Another change of fixture format for 1902/03 resulted in a two-division set up. This was to be Halifax's greatest-ever season, with the team not only taking the Division One title, but also winning the Challenge Cup for their only ever 'double'. Here, captains Archie Rigg and Jim Lomas (Salford) toss up ahead of the Cup Final at Headingley.

An unsigned painting which purports to show action from the 1902/03 Challenge Cup final, which was won 7-0 by Halifax.

The 1902/03 'double' winners. From left to right, back row: Summerskill, Winskill, Ricketts (secretary), Little, Tyson (president), Jack Riley, Dickenson. Third row: Bartle, Hadwen, Joe Riley, Rigg, W.W. Williams, Wedgwood, H. Wilson. Second row: Jones, Brown, Nettleton, Kitson, J. Morley, Mallinson, Swinbank. Front row: Midgley, Hammond, Bulmer, Morton, Langhorn, Morris.

The climax of the 1902/03 season was a hectic time for the players. After the Cup Final on Saturday 25 April, there was the crucial final league match on the Monday at Leigh, which Halifax duly won 11-0. The players were given a four-page programme to remind them of where and when they needed to be.

THE HALIFAX CRICKET & FOOTBALL CLUB
YORKSHIRE

Time Table

AND

PROGRAMME,

FOR

SATURDAY, SUNDAY, and MONDAY,

APRIL 25TH, 26TH AND 27TH, 1903.

WILD, HX.

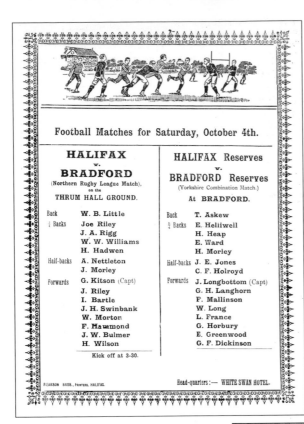

Football Matches for Saturday, October 4th.

HALIFAX		HALIFAX Reserves	
v.		v.	
BRADFORD		BRADFORD Reserves	
(Northern Rugby League Match),		(Yorkshire Combination Match.)	
on the			
THRUM HALL GROUND.		At BRADFORD.	
Back	W. B. Little	Back	T. Askew
¾ Backs	Joe Riley	¾ Backs	E. Helliwell
	J. A. Rigg		H. Heap
	W. W. Williams		E. Ward
	H. Hadwen		H. Morley
Half-backs	A. Nettleton	Half-backs	J. E. Jones
	J. Morley		C. F. Holroyd
Forwards	G. Kitson (Capt)	Forwards	J. Longbottom (Capt)
	J. Riley		G. H. Langhorn
	I. Bartle		F. Mallinson
	J. H. Swinbank		W. Long
	W. Morton		L. France
	F. Hammond		G. Horbury
	J. W. Bulmer		E. Greenwood
	H. Wilson		G. F. Dickinson

Kick off at 3-30.

PEARSON BROS., PRINTERS, HALIFAX.   Head-quarters :— WHITE SWAN HOTEL.

In these days before the advent of matchday programmes, clubs often issued team sheets, which might be circulated around the area prior to the game for publicity purposes. This example from 1902 advertises matches that were won 9-0 (first team) and 14-6 (reserves).

George Kitson, the captain in 1902/03 (although he missed the Cup Final through injury) had played for the club since its Rugby Union days in 1894. His sons John (in the 1920s) and Harry (in the 1930s) also represented the club.

Halifax won the Challenge Cup again in 1903/04, these newspaper illustrations from the final against Warrington at Salford including the two Halifax tries, by Joe Riley and skipper Johnny Morley, in an 8-3 triumph.

HALIFAX RETAIN THE CUP

Joe Riley gets over for Halifax

Morley interrupts the progress of Fish

The Referee gets in the line of play.

Hallam outwits the Halifax attack

Morley slips through the scrum and scores.

● An artist's impression of the 1904 final in which Halifax beat Warrington 8-3 at Salford

On their return to Thrum Hall, the victorious squad were photographed with the trophy, and a few young admirers, on the cricket field. From left to right, back row: Naylor, Jack Riley, Spencer, Langhorn, Hammond, Ricketts, Little, Winskill, Joe Riley. Middle row: Mallinson, Bartle, J. Morley, Rigg, Butler, Wedgwood, Morton. Front row: Midgley, Nettleton, Gledhill, Hadwen, Hartley, Morris.

Clubs reverted to a single-league system in 1905/06, following the abandonment of the two divisions, Halifax finishing ninth. From left to right, back row: Swinbank, W.W. Williams, Hammond, Langhorn, Ricketts, Wedgwood, Robinson, Mallinson, Morton. Middle row: Midgley, Grey, H. Wilson, Little, Ward, Hartley, Joe Riley, Morris. Front row: H. Morley, Hilton, Lewis, Cottam, Eccles, Brearley.

The glory days were back in 1906/07 when Halifax finished top of the league, then became the winners of the new top four play-offs. The scoreboard displays the result of the Championship final against Oldham. From left to right, back row: Midgley, W.W. Williams, Wedgwood, T.S. Dodd (president), Bulmer, Ricketts, Robinson, Bartle, Brearley, Foster, Morris. Middle row: Swinbank, Atkins, Littlewood, Joe Riley, Langhorn, W.J. Williams, Ward, H. Morley. Front row: Grey, Hilton, Eccles.

One of several postcards produced in 1906/07 depicting lucky-mascot Smut. The stray black cat had appeared in the pavilion on 17 November and heralded a run of 17 games without defeat, sending the team to the top of the league. This card was issued after Halifax were finally beaten on 23 February at Salford.

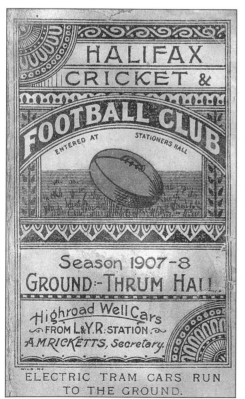

Fixture cards were issued by the club each season. This example is from 1907/08, a season of serious financial strife with recorded losses of £513. An appeal fund was launched, the Lord Mayor showing his sympathy by donating £100.

Following experiments with programmes for special testimonial games, Halifax became one of the first clubs to introduce a regular matchday programme. Number one was for the Yorkshire Cup first round match against Leeds on 10 October 1908. Halifax won 13-0.

The team went on to win the Yorkshire Cup in 1908/09, and also won the Yorkshire League trophy, instituted the previous season when they had been runners-up. From left to right, back row: Atkins, Medley, Swinbank, H. Morley. Third row: Ricketts, Ward, Sunderland, Brearley, Mallinson, Proctor, Little, Joe Riley, Foster, Mackay (trainer). Second row: Robinson, Hammond, Littlewood, Wedgwood, Langhorn, Thomas, W.J. Williams. Front row: Grey, Hilton.

Jimmy Hilton, a half-back signed from Leigh who made 234 appearances for the Blue and Whites between 1904 and 1912 before being sold to Wigan. He was said to be 5ft 2ins tall and weighed 10½ stones.

Hilton's half-back partner between 1906 and 1910 was Welshman Tommy Grey, who joined the club from Swansea. By the time this cigarette card appeared in 1911, however, he was a Huddersfield player, helping them to the league Championship in both 1911/12 and 1912/13.

Billy Williams was a Welsh flier who, in 1908/09, scored a (then) club record 45 tries in 39 matches on the wing. Another four tries in representative matches gave him 49 for the season, a new record for the Northern Union. In all he registered 113 tries for Halifax in 147 games.

Jack Swinbank was a policeman who became the stalwart of a mighty Halifax pack for a decade after arriving from Clayton, the Bradford-based amateur side, in 1900. The photograph shows him wearing the shirt and cap of the Yorkshire County side, for whom he appeared four times in the 1903/04 season.

The successes of earlier seasons became fading memories in the years leading up to the First World War. In 1909/10 Halifax finished ninth. From left to right, back row: Medley, Littlewood, Little, Ricketts, Brearley, Mallinson, Langhorn, Crabtree, Cottam, Hickling (trainer). Middle row: Ward, H. Morley, Grey, Hammond, Joe Riley, W.J. Williams, Robinson. Front row: Hilton, Eccles.

Halifax fielded a strong contingent of Welsh players in this period. Stuart Prosser (left) signed in 1912, with Welsh Rugby Union international Bobby Lloyd and winger Tom Robbins (right) following in 1914, all from Pontypool Rugby Union Club. Robbins stayed for only one season, but Prosser and Lloyd formed a long-standing half-back partnership, and both won selection for Great Britain tours.

The players may not have been full-time professionals, but some were given jobs working on the ground. Shown here in 1914 with an assortment of rakes, scythes and brushes are, from left to right, back row: Evans, Beames, Griffiths, Paterson. Middle row: Burgham, Jenkins, Brown. Front row: Fairfax, Lloyd, Ewart, Rigg. The Main Stand behind them had been opened in 1911.

The same group pose with one of the sheep owned by Messrs Tordoff and Longbottom who, according to the minute book, had paid £1 for them to graze on the football field during the summer of 1914. The previous April, the ground had hosted the Challenge Cup final between Hull and Wakefield Trinity.

John Ewart, a Scotsman brought south from Selkirk Rugby Union Club in 1914. He was to play only five first team games before he went away to fight in the First World War with the Cameron Highlanders. Sadly, he never returned.

REES (HALIFAX FOOTBALL CLUB).

Ned Rees, a half-back who made 95 appearances between 1911 and 1915. He was recruited from Merthyr Tydfil, one of a handful of Welsh clubs admitted to the league in a futile attempt at expansion.

Tommy Griffiths, a Welsh three-quarter who scored 10 tries and 26 goals in 30 first team appearances between 1913 and 1915. The blazer and cap are those of Newport Rugby Club.

Two of the leading players of the period were Jack Beames and Frank Williams. Both their careers spanned the years 1913 to 1923, and both won international honours with Great Britain. Williams, along with Stuart Prosser, had played in the famous 'Rorke's Drift' test match in Australia in 1914, and he later became the sports editor of the *Halifax Courier*, reporting for many years on the fortunes of his former club.

As well as the club itself issuing fixture lists, they were also produced by some of the town's pubs. This 1914/15 card came from the Corporation Inn, whose landlord was former player Herbert Hadwen. Hadwen, previously with Salford, had joined Halifax in 1902 from Morecambe, who at that time played in the Second Division.

By the time this photograph was taken in 1914, war had been declared with Germany. However, as a widespread belief that it would be all over by Christmas prevailed, the game carried on as normal. Halifax climbed to eighth in the table, their best finish since 1909. From left to right, back row: Beames, Prosser, Lloyd, Burgham. Middle row: unknown, Latham (secretary), Sherwood, Garforth, Longworth, Evans, Robinson, Brown, Fairfax, Rigg (trainer), Lingard. Front row: Metcalfe, Griffiths, F. Williams, Joe Riley, Jenkins, Ewart, Paterson.

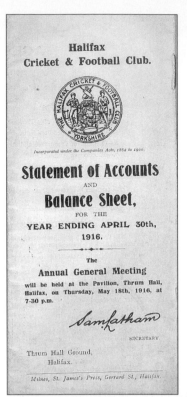

Halifax
Cricket & Football Club.

Incorporated under the Companies Acts, 1862 to 1900.

Statement of Accounts
AND
Balance Sheet,
FOR THE
YEAR ENDING APRIL 30th,
1916.

The
Annual General Meeting
will be held at the Pavilion, Thrum Hall,
Halifax, on Thursday, May 18th, 1916, at
7-30 p.m.

Sam Latham

SECRETARY

Thrum Hall Ground,
Halifax.

Milnes, St. James's Press, Gerrard St., Halifax.

When it became clear the war would continue for some time, the clubs agreed in 1915 that competitive football would end for its duration. Halifax continued to play friendly matches on a regular basis, with the players unpaid. The balance sheet for 1915/16 still revealed a loss of £112.

One or two of the friendly matches were under Rugby Union rules. On Christmas Day 1917, the Halifax team shown here turned out against the Devonport Royal Navy Depot touring team, losing 25-0. Under the captaincy of Jack Beames (with the ball), the side was: Metcalfe, Noble, Todd, Robertshaw, Stacey, Pemberton, Beames, Holmes, Milnes, Schofield, Sherwood, Whitehouse, Mattock, Sutcliffe, Roberts.

40

Three
Between the Wars

A view of the Thrum Hall ground in June 1919 on the occasion of a United Sunday Schools Peace Commemoration, when children from local Sunday schools gathered to sing hymns and say prayers in thankfulness that the horrors of the First World War were over. The Main Stand on the left was still the only cover available to spectators.

Clem Garforth was a full-back or three-quarter who had cost £200 from Batley in 1918, although he was a local lad who had earlier appeared for Halifax Town Association Football Club. Indeed, he had played for Halifax Town in their first-ever match in September 1911. He starred across town at Thrum Hall until 1925, and later became a popular publican in the area.

Alf Milnes, born in Mytholmroyd, joined Halifax from Sowerby Bridge Free Wanderers in 1915 and went on to represent his home-town club for ten years, scoring 10 tries and 3 goals in 174 appearances. He was selected for the 1920 Great Britain Tour, playing in two test matches against Australia.

The team of 1919/20 which finished sixth in the table. From left to right, back row: unknown, S. Foster, Broadbent, Gibson, Whiteley, Milnes, Garforth, Todd, unknown, Heyhurst (trainer). Middle row: Beames, Robinson, Lingard, Stacey, Lloyd. Front row: Turnbull, Prosser, Akroyd.

Sporting their Sunday best, and what in two cases appear to be medals, are Albert Akroyd, Jack Beames and Archie Clegg. Akroyd, a centre between 1910 and 1923, and Clegg, a centre from 1919 to 1921, were locals, while Beames was from Wales.

Halifax cashed in on the post-war boom in the 1920/21 season when they were Yorkshire League champions for the first time since 1909. They also reached the Challenge Cup final, but were surprisingly beaten 13-0 by Leigh. From left to right, back row: Rawbone, Broadbent, Milnes, Rushworth, Foster, Gledhill, Beames, Kitson, Rees. Front row: Turnbull, Todd, Schofield, Akroyd, Stacey, Whitaker, Robinson, Hirst.

The programme for the 1921 Challenge Cup final was produced by the Broughton Rangers club, on whose ground at The Cliff, Lower Broughton Road, the match was played. The Cliff was later bought by Manchester United as a training ground.

In 1923, Godfrey Phillips Ltd produced a new brand of cigarettes called 'Pinnace'. To promote them, they began a series of soccer and rugby player cards, which numbered 2,462 in all. Thirteen of these were Halifax Rugby League players. Joe Gledhill, number 1,032, had played for Hunslet before the war, but joined his home-town club in 1919 and played 47 matches in the pack.

Frank Todd, card number 1,037, was also Halifax-born. Signing from the Pineberry amateur club he made his debut in 1916, played in a number of wartime friendly fixtures, then made 333 official appearances for Halifax. He won 3 international caps for England and 8 for Yorkshire as a centre, wing and half-back. His son Brian played for Halifax in the 1960s.

45

Throughout the period between the wars, the Halifax matchday programme was always one of the best in the game, with some attractive cover designs. The drawing on the front of the 1926/27 programmes was by J.J. Mulroy, an artist for the *Halifax Courier*.

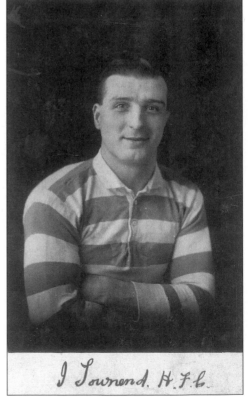

Irvine Townend, a £200 buy from Bradford Northern, made 201 appearances (32 tries) as a loose forward between 1923 and 1930. This postcard was one of thirteen produced for sale by the newly-formed Supporters' Club, which had started in June 1923.

'Candy' Evans (standing), Andrew Murdison and Jock Beattie take a break from training in October 1925 to congratulate Mr W.H. Wood, then aged seventy-eight, who was celebrating being connected with the Thrum Hall club for fifty years.

R. L. CUP - TIE,
1st ROUND.
Feb. 11th, 1928.
HALIFAX. v. HUNSLET.

HALIFAX. (Selected From)

1| DAVIES.
2| STACEY. 3| MURDISON.
4| KITSON.
5| SMITH 6| HAIGH
7| TODD.
8| GLEDHILL.
9| RAWBONE.
10| SWAN
11 HALLIDAY. 12| EVANS. 13| DOUGLAS.
14| BEATTIE. 15| TOWNEND.

HUNSLET.

1| PLACE.
2| BROUGHTON.
3| WALKINGTON.
4| NICHOLSON. 5| BEVERLEY. 6) COULSON.
7| YOUNG.
8| LITT. 9| WHITE
10| JENKINS. 11 CROWTHER
12| GUERIN.
13| DAWSON.

PHOTOS. HALIFAX COURIER.

The *Halifax Courier* issued a postcard for the Challenge Cup first round tie against Hunslet in 1927/28. The match ended in a 4-4 draw and, although the replay was won 16-2, Halifax lost at home to Swinton 3-2 in the second round. This was a disappointing period for the club, who had slipped to mid-table mediocrity.

The Halifax team that took on Huddersfield in the Yorkshire Cup first round in October 1928, losing 8-5. From left to right, back row: H. Smith, W. Smith, Haigh, Halliday, Evans, Swan, Rawbone. Front row: Townend, M. Smith, Rhoades, Stacey, Hanson, R. Davies.

Halifax's only try of the Huddersfield match, about to be scored by second-row forward George Swan. As can be seen in this and the team photograph, crowds were often huge at the time (23,000 for this match) despite the team's relative lack of success.

Spectators in the Main Stand and paddock area in the late 1920s, with piles of straw ready to protect the field from frost. The ground was highly-rated at this time. During the 1920s, three Challenge Cup semi-finals were played at Thrum Hall, whilst the Yorkshire Cup final was held there in 1921 and 1930, the Championship final in 1929 and 1930, and an international match was staged at the ground, also in 1930.

Full-back Dick Davies breaks through against Huddersfield. Between 1925 and 1928, the Welshman had a run of 105 consecutive first team appearances, a club record. Altogether he played 289 times between 1925 and 1933.

49

Action from a Halifax *v.* Hunslet match at Thrum Hall in January 1928, with the pavilion in the background still in its original style, complete with scoreboard and towers.

'Gillie' Hanson breaks from a scrum in the following season's fixture with Hunslet. Hanson, from Siddal, remained a popular figure in the town long after his retirement. The Hunslet player on the extreme left is 'Dolly' Dawson, later to become a very successful Halifax coach. This time the background shows the bottom side of the ground, which remained uncovered until the 1930s.

In the summer of 1928, the Supporters' Club organised a sevens tournament at Thrum Hall, featuring teams representing England, Scotland and Wales, plus a Harold Wagstaff VII. The winners, shown here, were Scotland, whose team of seven Halifax players consisted of: Swan, Beattie, Douglas (back row), Stacey, Renilson, Murdison and Hanson. Stacey and Hanson were locals, but the other five were genuine Scots. Although there had been a sevens tournament at Wigan in 1923, the event was described as 'novel', and attracted an attendance of 4,000.

In 1929/30, Halifax's second team finished top of their league for the first time ever, then beat York 'A' 13-5 in the Championship play-off final at Thrum Hall. Pictured here is the team which beat Hunslet 'A' in the final league game, with another healthy crowd present. From left to right, back row: Hirst, Whiteley, H. Chadwick, Swan, Whitehead, Holcroft, Caley, Wilson. Front row: Werrett, Roberts, W. Smith, Bright, D. Evans, Johnson.

Cigarette cards continued to be popular during the 1920s and 1930s, Halifax being well represented. A set of famous rugby players issued by Ogden's in the 1920s included Andrew Murdison, the 'Flying Scotsman', who was a prolific-scoring three-quarter. In 174 appearances he scored 92 tries and 135 goals between 1923 and 1929.

In the 1930s Ogden's produced a series called 'Football Club Captains', comprising both soccer and Rugby League players. The Halifax captain at the time was Harold Thomas, a wingman previously at Leeds and York. He played 57 matches between 1933 and 1936, scoring 15 tries.

If the 1920s had been disappointing, the 1930s began well for Halifax. In 1929 the Rugby League authorities had decided to take the Challenge Cup final to Wembley, and Halifax got there in 1931, their opponents being York. Preparations for the big day included a visit to West End Golf Club.

Pictured on the cricket field (with the pavilion now shorn of its towers) in the week before the final, are, from left to right: Rees, Norcliffe, Newman, Renton, Rawnsley, Atkinson, Bland, Crabtree, Higgs, R. Davies, Adams, Haigh, Higgins, Brown, Hanson, I. Davies, Jenkins (trainer).

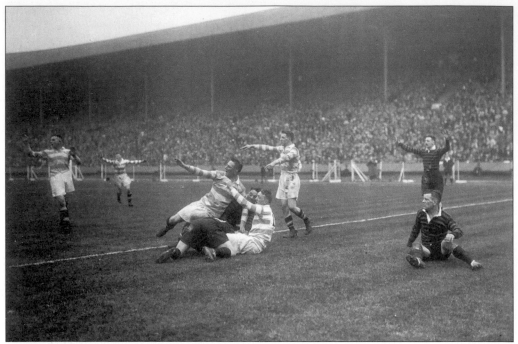

Decision time for referee Joe Eddon as Dai Rees, supported by nearest Halifax players Bland and Higgs, claims to have beaten the York defence to the touchdown. The score was ruled out, but tries for Bland, Ivor Davies and Higgins (2) did count as Halifax won 22-8.

The victory parade leaves Halifax railway station for the ascent of Horton Street on the way to a civic reception at the Town Hall. Crowds along the route were estimated at 100,000.

Caricatures of the Wembley players, including Lou Brown and Jimmy Gill who did not play in the final and excluding Fred Adams and Herbert Haigh who did, by Clifford Lees, more usually known for his nature scenes in the local newspaper.

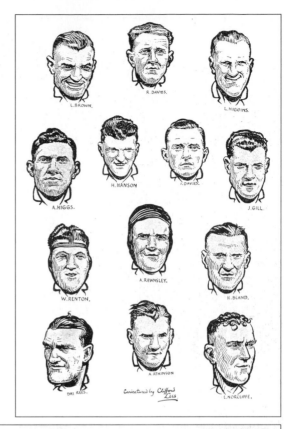

Players' autographs from the back of a menu card for a celebration dinner held at the Hotel Great Central, Marylebone, London, after the match.

Action from Mather Lane, Leigh's former home ground, in 1931, with Leigh hooker Fred Hilton attempting to hand-off Halifax winger Abe Johnson. Johnson went on to score a try and five goals in a 25-7 Halifax win.

This time the venue is Clarence Street, York, another ground no longer in use, as 'Gillie' Hanson and Herbert 'Tubby' Haigh end a York attack with Dai Rees ready to lend a hand or two.

'Tubby' Haigh evades the York defence at Thrum Hall. Haigh was a Halifax-born centre or stand-off who made 186 first team appearances between 1927 and 1934, scoring 25 tries.

Captains Dai Rees and Bryn Evans (Swinton) at Station Road, Swinton. Welshman Rees was described as one of the greatest generals the game has ever seen; he was a brilliant tactician, who was well respected by the players and able to bring the best out of them. He became a successful coach before returning to Thrum Hall as a director between 1961 and 1975.

Work on the ground was still being found for the players in the 1930s, particularly those brought up from Wales. Wooden flooring for the Bottom Stand was the priority in 1931, here occupying the attention of Lou Brown, Dai Evans, Dan Jenkins, Jackie Bright, Scotsman Jimmy Gill, Ivor Frowen and Dick Davies.

More toil ahead for the Welshmen, whose training shirts doubled as work-wear. The bottom side of the ground changed noticeably in the 1930s, with the roofing of the centre section of terracing. Having cost £1,260, the Bottom Stand was opened in 1934.

The 1932/33 season was a disappointment with the team down to twentieth, though shown here is the team that lost narrowly 16-11 at Wakefield in the Yorkshire Cup semi-final. From left to right, back row: Taylor, Higgs, Renton, Mitchell, Atkinson, Sparkes, Norcliffe, Newman. Front row: Jones, Maloney, Hanson, Haigh, Cutbush.

Special daytime training for a tough cup-tie away to league leaders Salford was halted for this photograph. Halifax, back up to fourth in this 1933/34 season, were optimistic and duly won 9-5, but lost in the next round at home to Widnes. From left to right, back row: (committeemen) Oates, Archbell, Webster, Wade, Lingard, Nuttall. Seated: Rees, Higgs, Atkinson, Renton, Morris, Cox, C. Davies, R.E. Thomas, Jones, Rule. Front row: Thornber, Gascoigne, Lockwood, H. Thomas, Sparkes, Webb (trainer).

A groggy George Todd leaves the field at Thrum Hall with the assistance of trainer William Bennett and the first aid men. Both Todd, an international stand-off signing from Hunslet, and Bennett, previously involved with Warrington, arrived in 1936 and served for a decade.

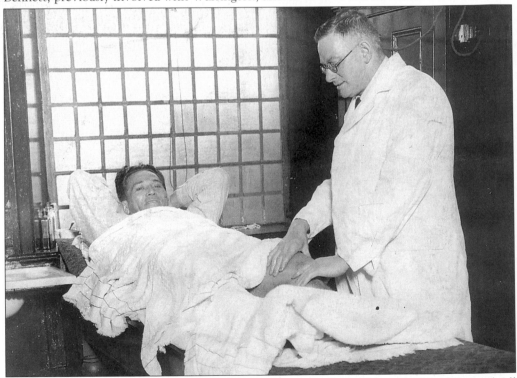

Bennett turns his hand to physiotherapy to treat the great George Nepia. A New Zealand All Black of some renown, Nepia joined Halifax from London club Streatham and Mitcham, but played only 13 matches (2 tries, 14 goals) before returning to his homeland.

Albert Atkinson, a stand-off or loose forward from Cumberland who settled in Halifax and gave great service to the club, first as a player (188 appearances, 33 tries, 2 goals) between 1927 and 1936, then as a trainer until his early death in 1953.

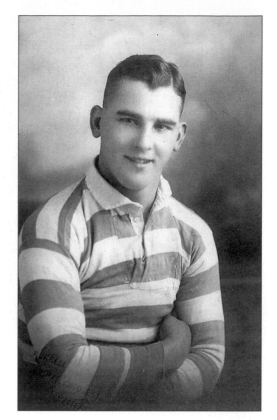

George Irving was signed in 1935 from Barrow to join his brother Hudson at Thrum Hall. Although he did not have the same impact as Hudson, he scored 5 tries in 25 first team appearances at stand-off in a stay of just over twelve months.

Full-back Hubert Lockwood in unflappable action at Wheldon Road, Castleford, in the late 1930s. Jack Goodall (right) and Charlie Smith are the other Halifax players in view. Lockwood became the first ever Halifax player to kick over 100 goals in a season, ending his Thrum Hall career in 1946 with 819 goals and 1,656 points.

Jack Cox appeals and the referee confirms that his second-row partner Hudson Irving has scored a try against St Helens at Thrum Hall. This was just one of many in Irving's long Halifax career (73 tries from 392 appearances – a record for a forward which has never been beaten).

Halifax's team for their first ever match in France in 1935/36. It was against Bordeaux, one of twelve founder clubs who had started Rugby League there in 1933. The match was played on Sunday 8 March, Halifax winning 40-25. The players, in these rather unusual shirts, are, from left to right, back row: Watson, Griffiths, H. Irving, Meek, Brindle, Baynham, Thornber. Front row: Hickey, Rule, Lockwood, R.E. Thomas, Sowden, Horrod.

New Year's Day 1939, and while one or two smile for the camera, the rest of the crowd packed on the terracing in front of the pavilion follow the enthralling action as Halifax beat Leeds 10-6.

Halifax were back at Wembley in 1939, New Zealander Charlie Smith here evading Salford's Gus Risman. Smith scored Halifax's first try in a thrilling 20-3 victory. Scrum-half Jack Goodall is the Halifax player in support.

A still from newsreel footage of the final shows Luddenden-based Jack Cox on his way to the try-line, having received a pass from his captain Harry Beverley. Sadly for Cox and Halifax the pass was ruled to be forward and the try was disallowed.

George Baynham and Jack Cox hoist the inspirational Harry Beverley on to their shoulders to begin the Wembley lap of honour. Other players shown, from left to right, are Jim Bevan, Hudson Irving (with the Cup base), Jack Treen (behind) and George Todd.

Back at Halifax station the following Monday evening, Harry Beverley and Hubert Lockwood show off the Cup ahead of the traditional celebration ride to the Town Hall. The coach behind them, with the open top, carried the players, while the rest of the official party travelled on the decorated corporation double-decker to the left.

Autographs of the 1939 Wembley players and reserves.

Caricatures of the 1939 heroes, as drawn by J.J. Mulroy. From left to right, back row: Lockwood, Smith, Bevan, Hickey. Middle row: Bassett, Goodall, Todd, Irving. Front row: Treen, Cox, Beverley, Field (behind), Baynham, J. Chadwick.

Halifax had been building a formidable side in the late 1930s and seemed on the verge of a great era, but the outbreak of war in 1939 brought the break-up of the team. The careers of many players were to be ruined. Here, young Welsh hopeful Idris Thomas, a recruit from Pontypool Rugby Union Club, meets trainer Bill Bennett and secretary-manager Arthur Archbell on his first day at Thrum Hall in 1938/39, but he was to play only 17 first team games.

Thomas (left) with playing colleagues Glyn Elias and 'Sonny' Roberts. Elias, a full-back or three-quarter, was able to play fairly regularly during the war years and totalled 110 appearances.

Four

The 1940s

The Halifax club continued to play regularly throughout the Second World War as it had done during the previous one. Often guest players were brought in from other clubs to make up for those serving in the Forces. One who played regularly was Widnes' all-time-great scrum-half Tommy McCue. Widnes closed down for the war years and several of their players turned out for the Thrum Hallers. McCue, seen here breaking from a scrum against Wakefield Trinity, appeared 132 times between 1940 and 1945.

Halifax, with a new club badge following their change to a limited company in 1936, sent this circular to all their registered players to check on availability for the 1940/41 season. Terms on offer ensured matches were taken more seriously than those held during the First World War.

Halifax Rugby League Football Club, Ltd.

Address all communications to the Secretary-Manager:
ARTHUR ARCHBELL.
Pavilion, Thrum Hall, Halifax.

Telephones: Office 61026.
Residence 4886.
Telegrams: 61026 Halifax.

Registered Office:
PAVILION, THRUM HALL, HALIFAX.

Aug 10th 1940.

Dear.

You will have seen in the Press that the Rugby League Council have decided to carry on with football for Season 1940-41.

The Minister of Supply has also requested that all Clubs should get their teams together for the benefit of the general public during the present crisis.

I should therefor be obliged if you would answer the following questions, and return to me not later than Thursday August 15th, to enable us to ascertain the number of players who are available.

The Council have also decided the following terms of payment. 25/- for a Win, or Draw away from home, and 15/- for a Lose, or Draw at home.

1. Will you be able to get off work on Saturday afternoons.   ---------------

2. Are you prepared to play in all available matches.   ---------------

3. Will you be able to train on Tuesday or Thursday evenings, or both.   ---------------

Yours faithfully

Arthur Archbell
Secretary Manager.

Charlie Smith was unable to play in the league matches in 1940/41, but did appear in the cup ties which were played after its conclusion. Halifax reached the final only to lose to Leeds at Odsal, as they were to do again in 1941/42. Smith is seen here breaking out of the pavilion corner against Dewsbury in a game played later in the war.

Hudson Irving in defensive mode in a wartime match against Bradford Northern. Behind him is the Bradford legend Trevor Foster and another of the Widnes guest players, loose forward Harry Millington.

Tommy McCue bursts through against Wigan in 1944. Arthur Bassett is the Halifax player on the left with Harry Millington towards the right. Intriguingly, the match is a Yorkshire Cup semi-final, Wigan being guests in the competition. Halifax won to reach the final for the second time during the war years, having been runners-up to Bradford in 1941/42.

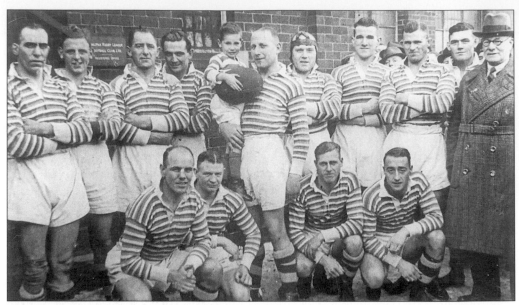

The Yorkshire Cup final team. It includes future St Helens star Alan Prescott, who was a seventeen year old winger in 1944, but went on to captain St Helens and Great Britain as a fearsome prop forward. From left to right, back row: McDowell, Prescott, Jones, Rule, Lockwood, Meek, Dixon, Irving, Millington. Front row: McCue, Todd, Bevan, Taylor.

The Yorkshire Cup final second-leg programme. Having already won the first leg at Hunslet 12-3, the 2-0 victory at Thrum Hall was merely icing on the cake. The programme was a typical Halifax issue of the time.

Halifax used their Yorkshire Cup final shirts on a number of occasions. The stripe was a mixture of two different shades of blue, a style often favoured by Halifax Rugby Union Club.

Fred Rule, who was available for most of the fixtures during the war, had signed for Halifax back in 1932 and did not play his last game until 1947. His 338 appearances as stand-off or centre brought him 92 tries and 8 goals.

A close-up of Harry Millington, who played 114 times for Halifax between 1940 and 1945, scoring 6 tries. He brought great experience to the side, having made an amazing 460 appearances for Widnes since 1928.

Half-back Danny Hurcombe registering one of his 17 Halifax tries in 92 appearances between 1937 and 1947. 'Danny' was a nickname because of his famous uncle of that name who had starred with Wigan and Great Britain before signing for Halifax in 1926. Both were born in Wales. Danny junior (real name Andrew) settled in Halifax and maintained an interest in the game as a coach and, later, Players Association official.

Normal operations resumed following the war in the 1945/46 season. Halifax fared only moderately, but crowds flocked to the matches, as can be seen in this view of the match against Bradford Northern. Loose forward Jack Dixon makes the drive after taking the ball from winger Arthur Daniels. Lancastrian Dixon played for Halifax between 1937 and 1947, scoring 33 tries in 220 appearances.

The team won the match against Bradford 20-0. From left to right, back row: Bassett, Meek, Smith, Dixon, T. Greenwood, W. Greenwood, Brereton. Front row: Mitchell, Lockwood, Rule, Daniels, Hurcombe, Humphrey.

'Goff' Humphrey, a Welsh centre or stand-off signed from Leicester Tigers Rugby Club, on the break against Featherstone Rovers at Thrum Hall in 1946. Prop Bill Greenwood is the player in support with Mel Meek in the background.

The Halifax team for the Infirmary Cup match against Huddersfield at Fartown in August 1946. It included a trialist scrum-half who played under the name of Whitfield, but was not signed. From left to right, back row: Day, Dixon, Brereton, Gronow, Smith, Nolan. Front row: Whitfield, Hurcombe, Dockar, Meek, Bevan, Humphrey, Chalkley.

Two Thrum Hall greats, Mel Meek and Charlie Smith, were granted a testimonial in 1947 for their long service. This was the cover for their testimonial brochure, the first of many issued by the club over the ensuing years. Above the action shots of the two players is a section of the Halifax support at Wembley in 1939.

Jack Dixon about to touch down for a try against Featherstone at Post Office Road. Bill Greenwood (grounded) and prop Frank Nolan are among those looking on.

Frank Mawson (left) watches as St Helens players McCormick, Whittaker (with the torn shorts) and Holland (7) upend Arthur Daniels.

Halifax did not have the greatest of sides in the forties, but in 1949 they shocked the Rugby League world by beating high-flying Huddersfield in the Challenge Cup semi-final at Odsal to reach Wembley for the third time. Here New Zealander Kia Rika (right) and Irishman Paddy Reid chase Huddersfield's Anderson at a packed Odsal Stadium.

A young Alvin Ackerley is halted in the same match. Frank Mawson (left) and prop John Rothwell are the other Halifax players nearby.

The 1949 Wembley squad displaying their new outfits. From left to right: Kielty, Kenny, Ackerley, Reid, Condon, F. Cox, Rothwell, Daniels, Rika, Price, E. MacDonald, Atkinson (trainer), Bennett (trainer), Mawson, Chalkley, Hatfield, Pansegrouw. The photograph also provides a rare view of the former scoreboard, which had to go when the terracing was extended backwards, and the former entrance to the pavilion's social club.

Michael Condon gets to grips with a Bradford opponent at Wembley to force a dropped ball. Frank Mawson is behind with Alvin Ackerley on the left.

Gareth Price was an inspired pre-Cup deadline signing from Leeds. Vastly experienced, the Welsh centre took over as captain and led his team to great effect. He was to stay for the following two seasons, scoring 22 tries in 87 appearances.

G.M. PRICE (CAPTAIN)

Price is standing ready to assist as Paddy Reid brings down Bradford Northern's Ernest Ward at Wembley. Stan Kielty is the other Halifax player close by.

John Rothwell's turn to get stuck in under the Wembley sunshine. Michael Condon (left) and Alvin Ackerley are also in shot.

Desperate Halifax defence prevents a Bradford try on this occasion, but Northern were to prove too strong on the day to win a disappointing final 12-0. Full-back Dennis Chalkley, Des Healy and Michael Condon are the Halifax players involved here.

Tragedy struck the club in the late 1940s. Cumbrian forward Hudson Irving died on the field in the match against Dewsbury on 12 April 1947, in his 392nd first team appearance. It was discovered at the inquest that Irving had a condition known as 'athlete's heart', although he had in fact died from a blood clot, accelerated by exertion.

Less than two years later, on 26 February 1949, flying winger David Craven, a Powderhall sprint finalist, dislocated his neck in a match against Workington. He died at the Royal Halifax Infirmary the following Thursday morning. The photograph shows Craven, a Durham lad who had scored 5 tries in 19 games, in typical sprinting style against Oldham. The Halifax players trying to keep up (in the lighter shirts) are Ike Proctor and Ken Ward.

Frank Cox, seen here taking the ball down the blind side against Widnes at Thrum Hall, was the brother of Jack Cox, but did not join Halifax until 1948, the year Jack died at just forty years of age. Both brothers were second-row forwards.

Harry Greenwood was the first of three generations of his family to play for Halifax. Sons Lee and Brett were followed by grandson Brandon in 1996. Harry made 132 appearances between 1946 and 1953 at loose forward or second row.

Five

The 1950s

Prop Don Hatfield is stopped by Leigh's Bill Kindon at Kirkhall Lane, the ground later to be renamed Hilton Park. Watching proceedings is speedy winger Hugh O'Connor, a recruit from local amateur side Asquiths.

The Halifax team at Dewsbury in January 1950. From left to right, back row: E. MacDonald, Rika, Olsen, Mawson, Hatfield, H. Greenwood, Ackerley, F. Cox. Front row: Kielty, Dean, Price, Chalkley, Daniels. The season finished with Halifax up to fourth place in the league table.

Signings for 1950/51 included Welsh Rugby Union international winger Terry Cook, but the team slipped to eleventh place. From left to right, back row: Hatfield, E. MacDonald, Wilkinson, Rika, Chalkley, Ackerley, Pearce, H. Greenwood. Front row: Kielty, Cook, Price, Dean, F. Cox.

Pre-season practice matches, with the squad split into two teams, could attract big crowds in this period. At half-time during this match in July 1950, the team in hooped shirts mingles with those in blue. Seen here are: F. Cox, Pearce, White, Olsen, O'Connor, Atkinson (trainer), H. Greenwood, Chalkley, E. MacDonald.

The crowd at the scoreboard end in 1950. It includes Arthur Daniels, who had returned home early through injury from Great Britain's tour to Australia. Although he was now fit again, he was barred from playing until the rest of the tourists arrived home.

Giant loose forward Frank Birkin breaks through against the New Zealand tourists in 1951, as blazer-clad referee Matt Coates looks on. Halifax won 18-12, one of the highlights of a disappointing season with the team down to twenty-first place.

Local recruit Vernon Halstead, who was a try-scorer in the match, watched by 15,000 spectators (if not the New Zealanders). The tourists were afterwards entertained to dinner at the Griffin Hotel at a cost of £54.

A try for Albert Fearnley at Bramley in 1952/53, as Halifax enter a new era of success with a surge up to second in the table. The other Halifax player shown is Welshman Bryn Hopkins, while among the massed Bramley ranks is former Thrum Haller Ike Proctor. Fearnley notched 38 tries for Halifax in his 207 appearances, but was noted more than anything for his work rate and prodigious tackling.

Dave Knopf, an Australian who had played Rugby Union in South Africa, took part in three trial games on the wing and at full-back in season 1953/54, but was not retained. Here he looks to off-load to Ken Dean on his debut against Doncaster, when he scored two tries.

Ken Adams' caricatures were regular features in the *Halifax Courier's Green Final*, the Saturday night sports paper, during the 1950s. This one shows scrum-half Stan Kielty, one of the club's best-ever players. Kielty holds the club appearance record of 482 between 1946 and 1958.

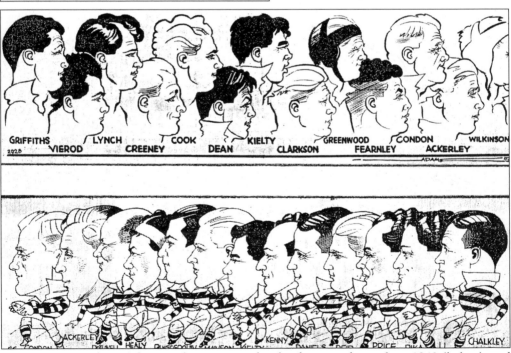

More caricatures from Adams, in his more usual style, showing players from 1949 (below), and the team who, in the 1952/53 season, reached the Championship final (above). The final was at Manchester City's Maine Road ground against St Helens, but Halifax lost 24-14.

A 1952/53 team group on the pavilion steps. From left to right, back row: Leeming, Fearnley, Thorley. Middle row: Hopkins, Ackerley, Bradley, Cook, Condon. Front row: Dean, Lawton, Daniels, Bowen, Lynch.

Famous West Indian world sprint champion McDonald Bailey visited Thrum Hall in 1953, meeting star players Ken Dean, Des Clarkson, Peter Todd, Alvin Ackerley and Stan Kielty. Bailey signed for Leigh in 1953/54, but played only a friendly match against Wigan.

Halifax topped the league in 1953/54 – the first time since 1906/07. This team played Hull in September without regulars Tuss Griffiths and Albert Fearnley, but won 15-11 in front of a crowd of 11,500. From left to right, back row: Lynch, Wilkinson, Daniels, Dawson (coach), Callighan, Clarkson, Pearce, Bradley, Thorley. Front row: Dean, Todd, Ackerley, Creeney, Kielty.

The return match at the Boulevard was scheduled for Monday 19 April, five days before Wembley. Not surprisingly, Halifax fielded their 'A' team. This blurred pocket camera photograph shows the team that lost 15-7. From left to right, back row: Rika, Hopkins, Vierod, Brant, Illingworth, Olsen, Pearce, Holmes, Broadhurst, Firth, J. Marchant. Front row: Mitchell, Pollard, Mather, Sykes, Briers.

Having won through to the Cup Final, Halifax met Warrington at Wembley. Here, Stan Kielty is introduced to Lord Derby by captain Alvin Ackerley. The other players, from left to right, are: Lynch, Bevan, Dean, Thorley, Wilkinson and Fearnley.

Second-rower Derrick Schofield, a signing from Rochdale Hornets the previous September, tangles with Warrington's Gerry Lowe on the Wembley turf. Stan Kielty hovers in the background.

Albert Fearnley, Stan Kielty, Alvin Ackerley and Peter Todd watch as Ken Dean heads for the try-line. He failed to make it, as did everyone else, in what was a drab 4-4 draw.

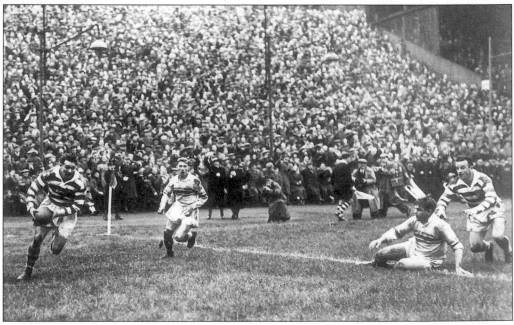

The replay at Odsal on Wednesday 5 May 1954 attracted a world record attendance, officially reported as 102,569, but it was to be a night of heartbreak for Halifax. This touchdown for Tommy Lynch was disallowed, as was a later effort by Arthur Daniels (pictured here extreme right) and Warrington won 8-4.

Three days later the same teams met at Maine Road in the Championship final, but Warrington, who had finished second to Halifax in the league table, won again, this time 8-7. Warrington ace Brian Bevan is here about to be tackled by his namesake Dai Bevan (extreme right).

The ball runs loose in the 1954/55 Yorkshire Cup final at Headingley when Halifax at last got their hands on some silverware by beating Hull 22-14. The Halifax players (dark shirts) in view are, from left to right: Griffiths, Thorley, Schofield, Fearnley, Dean, Wilkinson, Daniels and Palmer.

WEEKLY COURIER & GUARDIAN CUP-FINAL SOUVENIR

HALIFAX, SATURDAY, APRIL 28, 1956

Wembley beckoned again in 1955/56, the local newspaper issuing its usual Cup Final souvenir. From top left, clockwise, on the cover: Henderson, Wilkinson, Ackerley, Thorley, Schofield, Traill, Pearce, Bevan, Kielty, Dean, Daniels, Fearnley. In front are: Dawson, Lynch, Griffiths, Palmer and Freeman.

Chairman Ted Horsfall leads his players onto the field at Wembley, alongside opponents St Helens.

Jack Wilkinson is the central figure in this defensive action as the match gets underway. Ken Dean (6) and Arthur Daniels (2) are the potential reinforcements.

Former Halifax player Alan Prescott scores for St Helens in the last minute, despite the attentions of Tommy Lynch, to crown his team's 13-2 victory. Prescott won the Lance Todd trophy as man of the match, but for Halifax it was a third Challenge Cup final defeat in seven years.

Halifax had beaten Hull in the Yorkshire Cup final for a second successive season in 1955/56 (7-0 at Odsal) and, having finished second in the league, won through to meet them in the Championship final as well. Here Arthur Daniels, in an unfamiliar white shirt with blue chevron, scores one of Halifax's three tries.

Ken Dean is forced into touch by the corner flag as Johnny Freeman tries to lend a hand. Such a fourth try would have put Halifax clear, but when Hull's Colin Hutton kicked a last-second penalty goal, they were suddenly beaten 10-9, and had again missed out on a showpiece occasion.

Talented loose forward Ken Traill scores for Halifax against Leeds at Thrum Hall. Recruited from Bradford Northern in 1955, Traill was an exceptional handler of the ball and became the player who made the team tick. He made 90 appearances before being transferred to Wakefield in 1957.

Jimmy Lawton, a stand-off who was unlucky to be understudy to the great Ken Dean during the 1950s. This was one of a brace of tries he scored in 1957/58 against Batley, a team he soon afterwards joined and later captained. Charlie Renilson and John Burnett are in the background.

A try for Tommy Lynch in the Newstead corner at Thrum Hall, soon to be occupied by the Supporters' Club bar, which later became the Taverners' Club. The match is against Swinton, and the supporting Halifax player is Arthur Daniels.

The Newstead corner this time witnesses Derrick Schofield score against Dewsbury in September 1956. Schofield was filling in on the wing at the time, Andrew Turnbull having gone off in the twelfth minute of this pre-substitutes match.

Geoff Palmer, a big and powerful Cumbrian centre signed from Rosslyn Park Rugby Club, scored 99 tries in 209 appearances, but retired in 1961 for business reasons at just twenty-six years of age. The photograph shows him in action against Huddersfield and also includes (third left) Tommy Smales, who later joined the Halifax backroom staff as masseur.

Palmer breaks through against Bradford Northern, whose defenders include former Thrum Haller Arthur Daniels. The Halifax winger opposing Daniels is Johnny Freeman (right).

A familiar face behind the scenes at Thrum Hall for many years was bagman Bill Barrett, here seated in front of the paddock near the dugouts.

The end of a match at the Boulevard, with the Halifax and Hull players leaving the field all friends. John Thorley leads, with Albert Fearnley (left) and Brian Vierod behind. Thorley had been Halifax's sole representative in the Great Britain team that won the first World Cup tournament in France in 1954. He played 259 matches for Halifax between 1952 and 1960.

Halifax in 1956/57, a quiet season after the recent flurry of Cup Final appearances. From left to right, back row: Henderson, Traill, Palmer, Wilkinson, Thorley, Clifft, Pearce, Freeman, Dawson. Front row: Ackerley, Mather, Dean, Kielty, Broadhurst, Asquith, Owen.

The great 1950s team was breaking up, but there was a last period of success for the decade when Halifax were Yorkshire League Champions again in 1957/58. Pictured with the trophy, after the last home match of the season, are, from left to right, back row: Wynn, Wilkinson, Burnett, Snowden, Renilson, Jarman. Front row: Taylor, Lawton, Clifft, Williams.

The annual charity match against Huddersfield produced a scoreline of 37-35 in 1958/59. Keith Williams, who in one match the previous year had scored a club record eight tries, crossed for three more. From left to right, back row: Ramsden, Clifft, Wilkinson, Pearce, Sparks, Jarman, Burnett. Front row: Dean, Snowden, Palmer, Williams, Briers, Jones.

The Halifax team for the match at Hunslet in 1959/60. From left to right, back row: Sparks, Scroby, Critchley, Taylor, Thorley, Crabtree, F. Turnbull. Front row: Burnett, Owen, Snowden, Jones, Freeman, A. Marchant.

A section of the club record crowd of 29,153 who turned up for the match with Wigan in the Challenge Cup third round on 21 March 1959. The Halifax people amongst them went home disappointed as Wigan won 26-0.

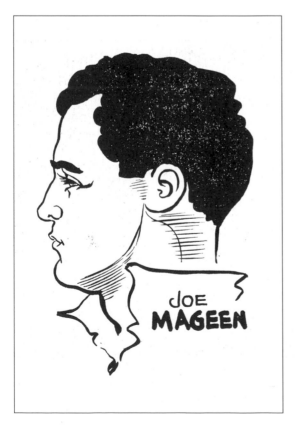

A Ken Adams caricature of centre Joe Mageen, a former Ovenden amateur player who was signed from Bradford Northern in 1957. He made 30 appearances, scoring 12 tries for his home-town club.

Six
1960-1974

The 1960/61 team headed the league table in December but, partly side-tracked by a run to the Challenge Cup semi-final, slid to thirteenth by the end of the campaign. From left to right, back row: Turnbull, Phillips, Fox, Renilson, Freeman, Snowden, Scroby, Burnett. Front row: Robinson, Marchant, Taylor, Owen, Palmer.

Full-back Garfield Owen in action at Thrum Hall, with Keith Williams in support. Owen was a former Welsh Rugby Union international who had signed for Halifax on BBC television's midweek sports programme *Sportsview*. A high quality goal-kicker and general player, he landed 535 goals in 166 appearances between 1956 and 1961.

Owen became the first winner of the Player of the Season award, inaugurated in 1960/61 by the Supporters' Club, who collected votes after every match. Geoff Palmer was runner-up. The trophy was handed over by the Supporters' Club president Fred Stringer.

For the 1962/63 season, the Rugby League experimented with a two-division system for the first time since 1905, Halifax qualifying for Division One. Some of the squad are shown at training with coaches Albert Fearnley and Stan Kielty (right). From left to right, back row: Fox, M. Williams, Hudson, Stevenson, Dixon, Jackson, Hardcastle, Kelley, Scott, Crabtree, trialist. Front row: Marchant, K. Williams, Robinson, Taylor, Rhodes, Fogerty, trialist, trialist.

Welsh players continued to figure prominently for the Blue and Whites. Here, three of them are side-by-side as Colin Dixon (left) and Johnny Freeman support a trademark break by Ronnie James. Eric Ashton is the Wigan player left trailing.

Johnny Freeman was one of Halifax's greatest ever wingmen, possessing both pace and skill in abundance. In 1956/57 he had established a club record of 48 tries in a season, and this 1960s effort was one of 290 in his career, another club record. International hooker John Shaw is also in view.

Colin Dixon began as a centre in the early sixties before going on to even greater success as an international forward. He is shown here taking the tackle as he puts wing partner Freeman away on another run. Half-backs Paul Daley and Barry Robinson are, as ever, in support.

Two significant new signings in the summer of 1963 helped put Halifax back on the Cup-winning trail. One was Ken Roberts, a £5,000 buy from Swinton. A great leader, he played 10 times for Great Britain during his relatively short four-year stint. Marking him at the play-the-ball in this 1965 photograph is Wakefield's Derek Turner.

The other important recruit was Alan Kellett, a former Ovenden amateur who had made a habit of scoring tries against Halifax while with Oldham. For this one at Watersheddings he leaves nearest challengers Peter Briers, Ken Dean (left) and Trevor Taylor (right) in his wake.

The Yorkshire Cup was back at Thrum Hall in 1963 after the 10-0 beating of Featherstone in the final at Belle Vue, Wakefield. With the Cup and bottles of Magnet Ale are Freeman, Jackson, Marchant, Fearnley (coach), Dixon, Burnett, Scroby, Robinson, Phillips, Renilson, Fox, Brown, Fogerty, Waddington (masseur), Roberts, Stacey (director), Hughes (secretary-manager).

Also in 1963/64, Halifax won the Eastern Division Championship, a tournament designed to maintain local derbies during the two-year period of divisional football. Castleford were beaten in the Fartown final, Halifax being presented with the former Yorkshire League trophy. From left to right, back row: Fogerty, James, Freeman, Burnett, Dixon, Marchant, Jackson, Robinson, Kellett, Renilson. Front row: Fearnley, Scott, Shaw.

The scrum has collapsed in a heap, but loose forward Charlie Renilson is as alert as ever to the danger and halts the progress of Hull KR scrum-half Dave Elliott at the old Craven Park ground in August 1964.

Jack Scroby was a mighty member of the 1960s pack, making 311 appearances in all, before later continuing his association with the club as coach and timekeeper. Here four Bradford forwards seem unlikely to succeed in putting him to ground.

Captains John Burnett and Alex Murphy (St Helens) lead out their teams for the 1965 Championship final at Station Road, Swinton. Halifax had finished seventh in the table, but stormed through to the Top Sixteen play-off final with some amazing late-season form. Behind Burnett are Ronnie James and Duncan Jackson.

Ronnie James powers into the St Helens defence, to be held on this occasion by Cliff Watson (10) and John Mantle. James was noted for his attacking play as well as his goal-kicking. He scored 45 tries and 1,028 goals for 2,191 points in his twelve seasons at Thrum Hall.

As the Saints players receive their runners-up medals, and the BBC television cameras switch off, Colin Dixon and Ken Roberts lift captain John Burnett on to their shoulders for the celebrations to commence. Halifax had won the match 15-7.

Halifax's spectacular football in the 1964/65 season enabled them to win the Mackeson Contest, awarded for the best average of points scored per match (Halifax averaged 18.66). John Burnett holds the trophy, and Albert Fearnley the Championship Cup, while most of the players and directors seem well on the way to having a good night.

The 1964/65 Championship winners line up back at Thrum Hall with the directors. From left to right: Bill Hughes (secretary-manager), Bill Boardall (director), Selwyn Heppenstall (director), Paul Daley, Hugh Duffy, Bernard Scott, Colin Dixon, Charlie Renilson, Jack Scroby, Ken Roberts, Alan Kellett, Ted Horsfall (chairman), John Burnett, Albert Fearnley (coach), Terry Fogerty, Barney Hardcastle, Johnny Freeman, Duncan Jackson, Brian Todd, Barry Robinson, Dave Harrison, Ronnie James, Bill Berry (director), Ron Ambler (director), Bill Stansfield (director) and former player Dai Rees (director). Todd and Duffy had been the two non-playing substitutes. This had been the first season that substitutes were allowed, but they could only replace an injured player and only up to half-time. Hardcastle and Scott had missed out on the final, but had been important fringe players, along with Stuart Kelley, Alan Rhodes, Dave Stockwell and Australian Lionel Williamson. The lattermost player was a young winger who never really settled at Thrum Hall, but went on to become an Australian international. Halifax continued to be blessed with a strong reserve side, which had added to the club's recent honours list by winning the Yorkshire Senior Competition championship in

1963/64. Albert Fearnley, following his highly-successful career as a player in the 1950s, had just become as prominent as a coach, later becoming a leading figure in the Rugby Football League's National Coaching Scheme. His tremendous enthusiasm for the game transmitted itself to the players, several of whom were to become coaches themselves in later years. Rugby League was still being played with unlimited tackles, prior to the introduction of the four-tackle rule in 1967/68 (increased to six in 1972), so Fearnley concentrated on building a powerful set of forwards as in the 1950s. Roberts, Fogerty, Dixon and Renilson all became Great Britain internationals in this period, while Scroby featured in the Yorkshire County side. Halifax were a successful side and entertaining to watch at this time, but attendances failed to attain the levels of earlier years. In 1964/65 they often struggled to reach 5,000, although there were 10,107 for the visit of Wigan in November. It was a problem faced by the game in general as people found alternative attractions on Saturday afternoons, and it sparked changes to the rules and a switch to Sunday football – in Halifax's case it also meant money troubles and a temporary halt to Cup success.

After winning the Championship play-offs from seventh place in 1964/65, Halifax almost topped it the following season, when they reached the final after finishing tenth. Unfortunately, St Helens gained revenge to the tune of 32-12. Halifax players and fans had their moment of glory in the semi-final when Wigan were beaten at Central Park, watched by a crowd of 23,292. Here, Terry Ramshaw tackles Eric Ashton, with Barrie Cooper also present.

Halifax were less successful in the Challenge Cup in the 1960s, a variety of gimmicks being tried in an attempt to improve performances. Here, Ian Crawshaw, Dave Rayner, Ronnie James and Barry Robinson sample a special health-improving bath.

Johnny Freeman was granted a benefit season in 1966/67, one of the highlights being a match against Keighley which attracted a crowd of 1,276. Pre-match formalities included introductions by Freeman to the Lord Mayor of Halifax. Lined up here, from left to right, are: Colin Dixon, David Jones, Peter Goodchild and Barrie Cooper.

Halifax were often invited into the annual seven-a-side competitions which were held for many years at Wigan and Leeds. In 1967 they won the Wigan event for the only time, the team being, from left to right: Robinson, Goodchild, S. Fearnley, Dixon, Renilson, James, Ramshaw.

The late 1960s saw the team on the slide again as star players moved on, although there were some good newcomers. This team group is from 1967/68. From left to right, back row: Michael, Eastwood, Hepworth, Fearnley, Mills, Howard, Dewhirst, Renilson, Nicholson. Front row: James, Goodchild, Dixon, Robinson, Jones, Pycroft.

Unusually, the cameraman moved indoors, snapping this group in the cricket club's ballroom in 1968. From left to right, back row: Giedziun, Halmshaw, Jones, Kirkbride, Crawshaw, Kelley, Fearnley, Probets, Renilson, Scroby. Front row: Goodchild, Reeves, Rayner, Kielty (coach), Dixon, Dean (coach), Baker, Robinson, B. Anderson.

Floodlights came to Thrum Hall in the 1967/68 season, at a cost of £8,524. They were officially switched on at the match on Friday 25 August against Widnes – appropriate in view of the wartime association between the clubs.

Thrum Hall, being the highest ground in the Rugby League, witnessed some dreadful playing conditions from time to time during the winter months. This scene from February 1970 shows, from left to right: Mike Kelly, Ronnie James, Gordon Baker, Stuart Kelley and Terry Fogerty leaving the field at half-time in a cup-tie against Swinton.

HALIFAX R.L.F.C.
Born 1873   Died 1970

An Appeal to the Public of Halifax
PLEASE DON'T LET
THRUM HALL DIE

Q. What can I do to help?

A. Please accept that the situation is critical and support the schemes put forward by the Appeal Committee.

There is a very grave danger that there will be no Halifax Rugby League Football Club to start next season - with your help this catastrophe can be avoided.

You could help in one or more of the following ways

1. Loan units, minimum £5, at 5 per cent interest, redeemable after five years.

2. Life membership at a cost of £50, any age, with a personal seat on main stand and including facilities of the pavilion. (Limited to 100 people).

3. Donations however small.

4. A Mile of Shillings is to be organised in the near future.

5. Volunteers will shortly distribute Paper Bags throughout the area to collect your woollen rags.

6. A sponsored walk or swim is to be organised.

Please Help

Enquiries :- Halifax R.L.F.C.   or   Rugby League Social Club
Halifax 61026   Halifax 61356

Halifax's financial situation worsened again in the late 1960s. The sale of Colin Dixon to Salford in December 1968 for a world record fee of £15,000 served only to reduce crowds and income, and another appeal fund had to be launched. This leaflet tried to show how grave the situation was.

Fund-raising events have been numerous over the years, but have not always been successful. The Halifax Pop and Blues Festival in 1970 was a huge flop when just 2,750 people turned up to an event which had cost £10,000 to stage and ended up merely adding to the club's debts.

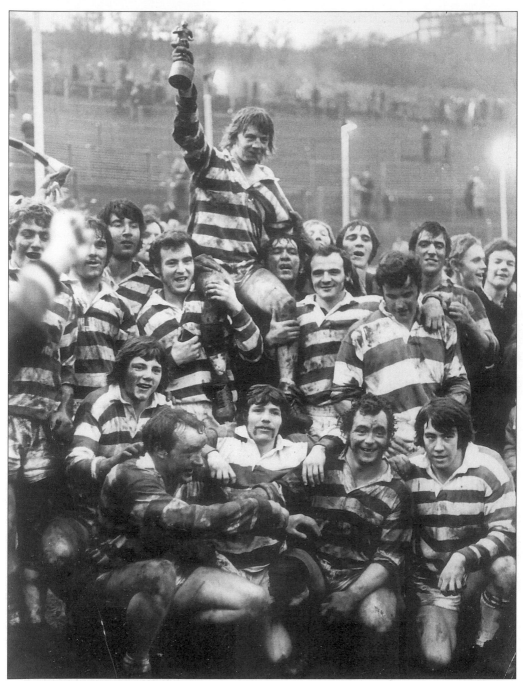

The crisis was survived and an influx of new directors helped bring new confidence to the club. In 1971/72 the team won through to the first-ever John Player final. Here, Gordon Baker and his team celebrate victory over Wakefield by 22-11 as a disappointing crowd of 8,295 quickly disperses. New shirts had been acquired for the final, but the players chose to wear the old ones from the previous rounds for luck. Only thirteen survived, so the substitutes wore the new ones. From left to right, back row: Halmshaw, Hepworth, Callon, Kelly, Baker, Dewhirst, Rayner, Davies, Reeves, Martin. Front row: Burton, Fogerty, Sanderson, Hawksley, Willicombe.

Player of the Season in 1971/72 was Tony Halmshaw (second left). The 'A' Team was in turmoil, barely able to raise a full complement of players and languishing at the bottom of the competition, but young forward David Shaw (fourth left) shone through to take that award. The Supporters' Club officials shown are Harry Robinson, Stuart Stott, Michael Agus and groundsman Granville Morton.

In 1972/73 Halifax finished eighteenth in the last season of one-division football. From left to right, back row: Wood, Fogerty, Tudball, Martin, Hawksley, Callon, Davies, Dewhirst, Willicombe. Front row: Kelly, Hepworth, Sanderson, Halmshaw, Baker, Brown.

Loose forward Tony Halmshaw was a skilful ball-handler who won international honours for Great Britain in 1971. Recruited from the Shaw Cross junior club in 1965, he served his apprenticeship in the reserves before playing 190 first team games. He was transferred to Rochdale in 1973 for £5,000.

Siddal product John Martin made his first team debut in 1967 and had gone on to total 262 matches (20 tries, 8 goals) by the time he moved on to Keighley in 1980. He was primarily a tough-tackling second-row forward, but also played at loose forward and prop forward.

David Jackson on the ball, backed by Terry Fogerty (centre) and Dave Callon, against Swinton in August 1973. The empty terracing behind, still unconcreted in 1973, reflected Halifax's status as a Division Two side. The attendance that day was 1,854.

Halifax went on to win promotion in 1973/74 and qualify for a complicated play-off competition that involved both First and Second Division sides. Here, Steve Brown (2), Phil Davies and Australian forward Mark Watson are in defensive action against Barrow.

The team which beat Huddersfield 35-26 in the pre-season Charity Match. From left to right, back row: Wright, Jackson, Martin, Callon, Hawksley, Davies, Booth, Baker, Musgrave. Front row: Williams, Burton, Hepworth, Fogerty, Brown, Pitchforth.

The match against Huyton in March attracted just 775 spectators, not many of them in view behind the team captained by starlet Bruce Burton. From left to right, back row: Price, Hoyle, Hawksley, Davies, Carlin, Dobson, Watson, Slattery, Baker. Front row: Sanderson, Shires, Burton, Pitchforth, Brown, Lewis.

Things certainly have not always run smoothly for Halifax. Here. Dave Callon falls foul of referee Eric Lawrenson as early as the ninth minute of a home match against Featherstone Rovers, seemingly the result of something he had said. The Rovers player is Barry Hollis.

Halifax completed their 100th season by taking part in the Wigan Sevens tournament again in the summer of 1974, but lost 23-6 to Wigan in the first round. From left to right, back row: Wilmot, Pitchforth, Hoyle, Davies. Front row: Dalgreen, Sanderson, Williams, Brown.

128